• NELL HILL'S •
Stylish Weddings

• NELL HILL'S •
Stylish Weddings

~ Mary Carol Garrity ~

Written by Micki Chestnut

With Michael J. Nolte
National Bridal Service Director of Wedding Planning Services

**Andrews McMeel
Publishing, LLC**
Kansas City

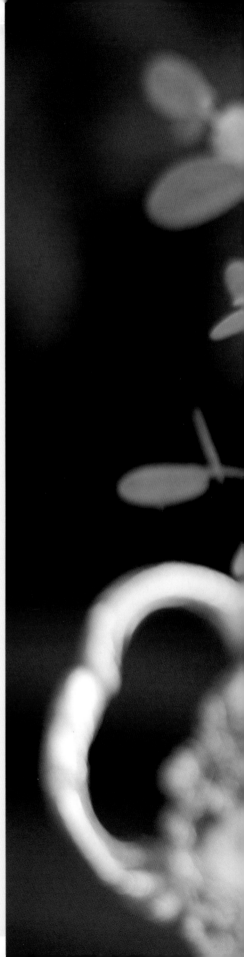

Developed by Jean Lowe,
River House Media, Inc., Leawood, Kansas

◦ NELL HILL'S ◦
Stylish Weddings

07 08 09 10 11 WKT 10 9 8 7 6 5 4 3 2 1
ISBN-13: 987-0-7407-6920-7
ISBN-10: 0-7407-6920-0

Library of Congress Control Number: 2007931351
Book design by Diane Marsh

Attention: Schools And Businesses

Andrews McMeel books are available at quantity discounts with bulk purchase
for educational, business, or sales promotional use. For information write Andrews
McMeel Publishing, LLC, 4520 Main Street, Kansas City, Missouri 64111.

Dedicated to Kelly and Britt

Contents

Introduction 9

Introduction

The other day, I was talking shop with a fellow MOB (mother of the bride), who shared stories about her daughter's recent wedding.

"What do you need when you're planning a dinner party?" she quizzed me.

"I don't know. What?" I inquired.

"Another hour!" she quipped.

"What do you need when you're planning a wedding?" she continued.

"I don't know. What?" I answered.

"Another week!" she said, and we both hooted, as only those who have experienced the agony and the ecstasy of planning a wedding can.

Before our daughter, Kelly, came home with an engagement ring on her left hand, I thought planning a wedding would be a breeze. After all, through the years, I've had a blast helping friends and family decorate for their big day. And at my home furnishings stores, I've worked with countless brides as they scout for everything from reception decorations to gifts for their bridal party.

Planning a wedding seemed like the perfect opportunity to do the two things I love more than life itself: decorate and host parties. What could be hard or stressful about that? I was soon to learn!

When Kelly shared that her childhood dream was to be married in our home, I was in heaven. I couldn't wait to create some wedding magic in our 130-year-old Greek revival. When we purchased our historic fixer-upper, our goal was to turn this money pit into a beloved family home that would witness the most wonderful moments of our lives. What could be more special than having Kelly's wedding here?

But as Kelly and I rolled up our sleeves and got to it, I was amazed by the amount of work hosting even a small wedding could be. Suddenly I could relate to all those stressed-out MOBs I'd worked with through the years.

Despite a few white-knuckle moments, like when rain pelted our courtyard hours before the garden reception began, Kelly's wedding turned out to be as magical as we dreamed. The time we spent together discussing everything from flowers to food brought Kelly and me even closer together. And I walked away brimming with dos and don'ts I couldn't wait to pass on to others who were just beginning their journey to this joyous celebration. That's how this book was born.

Nell Hill's Stylish Weddings is the kind of wedding guide I wish I had when planning Kelly's wedding. To help you avoid bumps and steer past pitfalls, I've filled the following pages with a host of practical tips, techniques, and insights from a panel of highly respected wedding professionals. You'll learn the secrets of planning an amazing celebration from a top wedding coordinator, discover how to create wedding and reception decorations that will dazzle your guests, and learn from the pros how to pick everything from stylish invitations to sumptuous reception fare.

I also invite you to join our family on our own wedding journey, from the moment my husband, Dan, and I toasted Kelly and Britt's engagement to the moment we waved good-bye to the happy bride and groom. So many friends and customers have asked about Kelly's wedding, so I'm excited to share all the delightful details and beautiful photos with you at last!

Since I learn so much from my creative friends and customers, I've also included ideas from a few weddings that were so beautiful they made my jaw drop. You'll learn how the brides arrived at their drop-dead-gorgeous color palettes and wove their weddings' signature looks into every detail of the events.

My hope is that after enjoying the practical tips and visual banquet we've prepared in *Nell Hill's Stylish Weddings*, you'll be less anxious and more excited about creating a once-in-a-lifetime celebration that honors the unique life and love of the bride and groom.

CHAPTER ONE

Congratulations!

Where Do You Begin?

On Thanksgiving Day, as Dan put the turkey in the oven, Britt, our daughter Kelly's longtime beau, let the cat out of the bag.

Britt had been antsy all day, trying to figure out how to get Dan alone so he could ask him a very important question. Britt had been around our family long enough to know that Kelly and I never venture near the kitchen while Dan's preparing a feast, so he knew it was the perfect place for a private audience. So it was amid the stuffing and mashed potatoes that Britt asked Dan for Kelly's hand in marriage.

Kelly and Britt met during her senior year in college. "He was cute and shy and you could just tell he was the nicest human ever," Kelly remembers. They started dating, then attended the same law school. We could tell the first time Kelly brought Britt to our home that he was the love of her life.

That's when we started Operation Wedding Watch. We didn't want to pry, asking insensitive questions like, "Are you two planning to get married?" So

I often begin parties at the front of my home in the foyer— where I set up extra bar service for arriving guests. For the wedding, we served Prosecco, a sparkling Italian wine, in champagne flutes as guests entered the front door.

instead, we lobbed out pathetically transparent queries like, "How are you and Britt doing?" as we'd scan her hand for an engagement ring.

Kelly admits she, too, was beginning to wonder when Britt would pop the question. Every time he took her out for a nice dinner, she'd get all dressed up, sure this was the night. Then one evening just before Christmas, after they dined at their favorite restaurant, Britt stopped on the sidewalk outside the restaurant, dropped to one knee, and asked her to be his wife.

That night, we got a call from our jubilant daughter, who couldn't wait to share her good news. On Christmas Day, when Kelly and Britt arrived at our home for our family celebration, we popped the cork on a chilled bottle of champagne and toasted the happy couple. A few minutes later, my sister, Judy, and I piled down Kelly with a stack of wedding books and magazines. We couldn't wait to start planning the big event!

❧ Decisions, Decisions ❧

The first big decision Kelly had to make—when to hold the wedding—turned out to be easy. She knew the upcoming year would be a busy one for her, between graduating from law school and starting a new job at a law firm. So she decided to hold her wedding during the only month she had off. August it would be.

For Kelly, the choice of where to hold the wedding was equally as clear. Ever since she was young, she'd dreamed of being married in our historic home. She shared with me that when she was a moony teenage girl, she imagined herself walking down our grand staircase to meet her groom at the bottom.

Then reality hit as she and Britt began to compile an ever-growing guest list. As Kelly put it, "The house was big, but not *wedding* big."

Discouraged, she and Britt considered other venues for their nuptials. They toyed with having a glamorous destination wedding, but the idea lost its luster when they realized few of their loved ones could join them on a

costly trip. I knew her heart was set on a home wedding, so together we resolved to make it work.

We did an honest assessment of how many guests we could fit in our home and garden, and then we faced the agonizing job of paring down the guest list to family and a few close friends. For me, taking names off the guest list was the hardest part of the entire event.

Kelly knew she wanted a short, simple service, so we decided the couple would exchange their vows in our entryway while guests looked on from the foyer. This would allow Kelly to make her long-anticipated entrance down the majestic staircase.

From the very beginning, Kelly knew she wanted her celebration to be more like an elegant dinner party than a wedding bash. She wanted a casual and relaxed, yet stylish and sophisticated, reception, where the focus was on fine food, good drinks, and excellent conversation. Nothing would do but a romantic candlelight dinner under the stars.

Bride: Kelly Garrity Bieri

Pink and Green

Since Kelly's wedding would be held during the hottest month of summer, she knew she wanted a color palette that was fresh and light. Because she is crazy about green, she knew tart apple had to be part of her palette. Once she paired this sassy color with hot pink, she'd found her look. With the color combination decided, we moved forward with our decorating plans, using pink and green as our primary palette. We opted for white as our table cover choice, but if you're looking for more ways to bring this palette to life in your plan, I've chosen some alternative fabric designs I think would go great with these bold hues.

XO   XO   XO

Here's To Love

Starter
Mushroom Velouté
followed by
Hearts of Romaine with Vinaigrette
to cleanse your palate
Raspberry Sorbet

entrée
*Grilled Alaskan Halibut
with Whole Grain Rice*
Asparagus La Roma
dessert
Markie's Chocolate Delight

Kelly &
April 8, 2006

A Family Affair

Soon after Kelly and Britt announced their engagement, Dan and I couldn't wait to get to know Kelly's future in-laws better. So we invited Britt's family over for a formal dinner to celebrate our children's upcoming union.

On a balmy night in early spring, Dr. Peter and Markie Bieri and their daughter, Kirsten, ventured to our home for an evening of pleasure and planning. Markie, who is a professional decorator, and my mom, Mary Lou Diebolt, walked with us through our home, ironing out a few of the logistics for the wedding.

To add a welcoming touch to our table, I wanted to treat our guests to a special surprise. A friend of mine suggested I make a keepsake that featured Kelly and Britt's photo. She helped me create a vellum overlay announcing Kelly and Britt's engagement, along with the dinner menu, and secured it to a darling photo of the couple, which we proud parents could save and frame. Dan prepared a fabulous feast for our celebration that included a main course of grilled Alaskan halibut, rice, and asparagus, followed by a rich chocolate dessert.

Drawing
on Experience

I don't consider myself a wedding planner, but by the time Kelly announced her engagement, I felt like a seasoned pro when it came to decorating for these happy events. As a retailer and interior decor enthusiast, during the last twenty-five years I've helped thousands of friends and customers come up with stylish decorations for bridal showers, luncheons, rehearsal dinners, ceremonies, and wedding receptions.

Since I enjoy creating over-the-top displays for my stores, seasonal open houses, and other events, friends and associates have asked me to help decorate for their children's weddings. Each time I've hosted or helped with an event, I've learned more about what works—and what doesn't. I knew this real-world knowledge would come in handy in planning Kelly's wedding.

My first request for wedding design services came from my friend Shirley, who needed help transforming a stark college cafeteria into a romantic garden reception for her son's wedding. To keep the guests' focus off the lackluster room, we decided to make the din-

ing tables the eye-catching focal point. First, we camouflaged the industrial-looking chairs by tying the tops with a few yards of scrim, a gauzy cotton fabric that's as inexpensive as it is romantic. We knotted the scrim at the back of the chair and then inserted a fresh sprig of lavender to add a touch of elegance. To spark up each table, we created a simple yet serene centerpiece of leggy ivy plants in adorable iron baskets surrounded by a sea of votives.

When my friend Cyreesa's daughter was married, I wanted to decorate the reception hall as my gift to the young couple. As it turned out, the party would be held in the same college cafeteria, one of the few venues available in our small town. I couldn't wait to go at this room again, trying out some new ideas to make it shine.

This time, I covered the utilitarian chairs with full slipcovers tied up with huge satin bows. To save time and money, we decided to rent the slip-covers from an event rental company instead of making our own. The chairs were magnificent, but I was shocked by how long it took us to dress each one. Here's the lesson I learned: If you don't have the time to invest in making plain chairs pretty, rent ballroom chairs. Since Cyreesa's event was a bit more formal than Shirley's had been, we made the centerpieces more elaborate and showy. We created multilevel displays with a variety of drop-dead-gorgeous crystal and silver pieces and then added in pops of green with ivy topiary.

By the time my niece Becca asked me to host her wedding reception at my home, I'd learned a lot from my previous wedding-decorating adventures. I was ready for a new challenge.

Becca's guest list was quite large, so we decided to hold the reception in our side yard. Since it invariably rains when I host an outdoor event, this time I got smart and rented a large event tent with a small dance floor. Sure enough, it poured and the ground beneath the tent turned into a soupy mess. By the end of the soggy evening, my brand-new shoes looked like they'd been through two hard summers.

Even though conditions outside the tent weren't optimal, inside every-thing was resplendent in crystal, silver, and candlelight. I came up with three different centerpiece treatments for the fifteen round tables that filled the tent.

I knew one treatment needed to be statuesque to help fill the cavernous space. So I added much-needed height and pulled in Becca's green and white color palette by placing live palm plants in large cache pots at the center of five tables. The graceful plants gave the space dramatic elegance. For the sec-ond centerpiece treatment, I wanted something of medium height, so I chose ornate silver candelabra surrounded by clusters of votives. The third group of tables needed to sport a more diminutive display, so I created a beautiful still life of flowers and bird figurines and covered it with a clear glass cloche.

TIPS FROM THE EXPERTS

For nearly thirty years, Michael Nolte has worked in almost every aspect of the wedding industry. As a wedding photographer, florist, and wedding attire specialist, he learned how to make wedding magic from the ground up. Today, Michael is a highly sought-after wedding coordinator, and his bridal salons, among the few to achieve National Bridal Service membership, are filled with couture wedding gowns and formalwear that will make you swoon.

Since Michael has helped hundreds of brides across the region achieve their dream weddings, I begged him to share his secrets with me. As he walked me through the ins and outs of planning a wedding, selecting attire, and creating checklists, I was amazed by his knowledge, practicality, and insight. I wish he had been by my side when we planned Kelly and Britt's wedding.

Some people love the challenge of pulling together a big event like a wedding. They enjoy doing the footwork, deciding each detail, and putting all the pieces together for a photo finish. For others, the months of hard work and nail-biting deadlines are akin to their worst nightmare.

Kelly and I decided not to use a wedding coordinator for a couple of reasons. Since the wedding would be the same size as parties we have hosted in our home, I knew exactly how to set up and decorate my house and garden. And, because I own home furnishings stores, I had access to lots of beautiful decorating pieces and loads of helpers that I wouldn't have otherwise. They saved the day!

But if Kelly's wedding had been any larger, or if I'd never before entertained to this magnitude in my home, I would have hired a wedding coordinator so fast it would have made your head spin. In my opinion, you can't beat having a seasoned pro by your side, giving you prudent advice at every turn and, best yet, shouldering the lion's share of the work.

PLANNING YOUR CELEBRATION

Tips from Michael Nolte

1 HIRE A WEDDING COORDINATOR, IF YOU'RE GOING TO USE ONE.

If you're considering hiring a coordinator for your wedding, here are a five considerations from Michael on how to find a great one:

❧ LOOK FOR CHEMISTRY. Since you will work so closely with your coordinator during what is typically a stressful period, make sure your match is made in heaven. Pick someone you're comfortable with, who cares about and respects your wishes, but who has enough take-charge professionalism to get the job done.

❧ LOOK FOR EXPERIENCE. How long has the coordinator been in the wedding business and what drew him or her to the field? It's best to pick someone with years of experience in several aspects of the wedding industry.

❧ PICK SOMEONE WHO HAS BEEN PROFESSION-ALLY TRAINED. Find a coordinator who has received training through the National Bridal Service, a hallmark of excellence in the wedding industry.

❧ ASK ABOUT FEES. Some wedding coordinators charge a percentage of the total wedding cost, with the industry average being 15 percent. Others charge an hourly rate, which averages about $150 per hour. Still others charge a flat rate. Be sure to find out how the coordinator charges before you reveal your wedding budget to ensure the fairest pricing possible.

❧ DETERMINE HOW ACCESSIBLE THE COORDINATOR IS TO CLIENTS. Is the coordinator on call 24/7, or do brides need to set up meetings weeks in advance? Find someone who will give you the amount of time and attention you're most comfortable with.

2 | SET A BUDGET.

Some brides know exactly what elements they want their weddings to include, such as a formal dinner or a live band, and they can adjust their budgets to fit their dreams. Others, like Kelly, have a set budget and must tailor their wedding plans to fit it. No matter what your situation, take heart. You can plan a beautiful wedding, even on a shoestring.

If you're not sure how to set an accurate budget, talk with your wedding coordinator about standard costs or with other wedding professionals, such as caterers, florists, or photographers, to see what they charge.

To help you figure, Michael says 50 percent of your budget will likely be devoted to food and beverages. Right now, the national average for a basic wedding for 200 guests is $30,000, a price that doesn't include extras like an open bar at the reception, a live band, or a wedding coordinator.

3 | BOOK THE VENUES FOR YOUR BIG DAY.

Kelly had a strong attachment to our home, so she knew this was the perfect spot for her ceremony.

❧ SELECT A CEREMONY SITE LOADED WITH SENTIMENT AND SIZED APPROPRIATELY.

Others may be sentimental about the house of worship they attended since childhood or the place their parents or grand-parents were married. Still others may have dreamed of being married at one of their city's favorite landmarks, like a historic home, a rose garden, or a popular cathedral.

Don't worry if your sentimental spot doesn't have fairy-tale ambience. A talented wedding coordinator or decorator can transform even the most ho-hum of venues into something extraordinary. The most important thing is to follow your heart.

Just like Goldilocks, you want to find a ceremony site that's not too big, not too little, but just right. All too often, brides are wooed by the thought of being married in majestic venues, forgetting how a cathedral that seats 1,200 will dwarf their party of 200 guests. But when you pick a venue that comfortably accommodates your guest list, the bride will feel the exhilaration of walking into a sea of well-wishers, not a cavern that's nearly empty.

However, if your heart is set on an oversize venue, Michael says there are tricks to make a big space seem cozier. For instance, ushers can seat guests up and down the center aisle so when the bride walks down the aisle, she's greeted at every pew by smiling faces.

❧ PICK THE RECEPTION VENUE THAT FITS YOU BEST.

Hotel ballrooms. Some brides think of hotel ballrooms as boring blank boxes, but Michael sees them as blank canvases on which to create a masterpiece. Add some marvelous

decorations and loads of candlelight, and they can be enchanting.

Historic homes or other historic sites. While these charming old venues have loads of character, you may need to camouflage areas that are well worn or in need of repair.

Country clubs. Private clubs are usually well appointed, but they often feature several smaller dining rooms instead of one grand ballroom. That means guests may not all fit to view highlights like the cutting of the cake or the first dance.

Private home. While private homes are a sentimental favorite of Michael's, he concedes that most homes aren't large enough to accommodate a wedding guest list. He also cautions that when the bride's family hosts the wedding and reception in their own home, it puts additional strain on them during an already busy time.

Garden. Gardens are Michael's all-time favorite spot for a wedding reception, but he notes that garden celebrations can also be the most expensive. If you opt for an outdoor reception, you must go in planning for rain, he says, renting a tent with sidewalls, flooring, and gutters, so you aren't caught off guard if the weather turns foul.

Fraternal lodge or church fellowship hall. While these venues offer ample space, they often lack the stylish ambience most brides want for their wedding receptions. But Michael says there are plenty of tricks of the trade for making even the roughest of rooms feel romantic. For instance, you can drape the walls with fabric, cut the lights and use scores of candles, and upgrade the tables and chairs.

4 HIRE YOUR PROFESSIONAL TEAM.

Now it's time to hire your dream team, the florist, photographer, caterer, and other wedding professionals who will make your wedding sublime. We'll give you some pointers on how to pick the pros in chapter 2.

5 CHOOSE A WEDDING DRESS.

The bride's gown sets the tone and feel for the entire wedding, so it's important she finds a gown so rapturous, it brings tears to her—and everyone else's—eyes. When you begin shopping for bridal gowns, avoid what Michael calls the "Velcro approach"— throwing a wide array of gown styles at the bride until one of them "sticks." Instead, he encourages brides to approach gown shopping very thoughtfully and deliberately, keeping these tips in mind:

❧ NAME THREE ADJECTIVES YOU WANT TO DESCRIBE YOUR WEDDING. Do you want your wedding to be romantic? Elegant? Casual? Fun? Each of these descriptors dictates an entirely different kind of dress.

❧ PICTURE THE GOWN AT YOUR VENUE. If you're getting married in a huge cathedral with a long aisle, you'll want a dress with a long train. But if your wedding will be held in a garden, you don't want a train at all, or a very small one.

🌿 CONSIDER THE SIZE OF YOUR WEDDING. If the wedding is huge, the bride needs a dress that makes a big statement so she won't get lost in the crowd.

🌿 FIND A STYLE THAT FITS WELL WITH YOUR BODY TYPE. No matter what your shape, there's a wedding dress out there that will make you look like a princess. Be guided more by finding lines that flatter your figure than by the latest trends.

🌿 CONSIDER THE SEASON AND TIME OF DAY. While wedding dress designers no longer offer separate spring/summer and fall/winter lines, you still want a dress that doesn't look out of place for the time of year and time of day.

🌿 DON'T FORGET THE VEIL. Michael is passionate about veils because he believes that a veil is what makes a bride a bride. Without a veil, he insists, she's just a woman in a white dress. He's seen the magical transformation happen again and again in the dressing rooms of his salons. When a bride tries on a wedding gown, her mother smiles. But when Michael adds the veil, Mom starts to weep.

DRESSED TO DAZZLE

✣ BRIDESMAIDS. In order for the bridesmaids' dresses to complement but not compete with the bride, they must have two elements in common with the bridal gown, such as the neckline, skirt style, fabric, and embellishments. Remember that wedding guests will view the wedding party from behind for the majority of the service, so it's important to select dresses that have a fabulous back view.

✣ MOTHER OF THE BRIDE AND MOTHER OF THE GROOM. Etiquette dictates that the mother of the bride sets the fashion tone for the parents' attire. The mother of the groom's dress should mirror the length and style of that worn by the mother of the bride. But the old rule that says the mothers' dresses must match the colors worn by the brides-maids has gone by the wayside, as has the idea that a short dress should be worn for a day wedding and a long dress for an evening ceremony. Michael suggests that mothers wear any style and color that makes them feel beautiful, whether it's a formal gown or a business cocktail suit.

✣ FLOWER GIRLS. While the flower girl's dress doesn't need to match the bridal gown, it does need to blend well with the dresses worn by the bride and bridesmaids. The key is to keep the dress age-appropriate so the flower girl looks like an enchanting fairy, not a little girl in a big girl's dress.

✣ RING BEARER. The ring bearer can wear either a tuxedo that matches the groomsmen's or a pageboy outfit, which consists of short pants, knee socks, and saddle oxfords.

MEN'S FORMALWEAR MADE EASY

While formalwear companies may encourage a look that reflects the latest trends, Michael strongly urges men to stick with traditional formal attire. It looks classic and clean and will never go out of style, so the groom won't have to worry about his future children laughing at his wedding photos, saying, "Dad, I can't believe you wore *that*!" Tradition dictates exactly what men should wear based on the formality of the event and the time of day the event will be held.

DAYTIME WEDDINGS
(HELD BEFORE 6 P.M.)

Ultraformal:
◇ Cutaway coat
◇ Hickory stripe trouser
◇ Pearl gray vest
◇ Ascot
◇ Gray gloves

Formal:
◇ Stroller jacket
◇ Hickory stripe trouser
◇ Gray vest
◇ Windsor tie or four-in-hand tie

EVENING WEDDINGS
(HELD AFTER 6:00 P.M.)

Ultraformal:
◇ Black tailcoat
◇ White pique shirt
◇ White shirt studs
◇ White pique tie
◇ White pique vest
◇ White gloves

Formal:
◇ Black square-cut tuxedo, single- or double-breasted
◇ Bow tie or Windsor tie
◇ Cummerbund or vest
◇ White shirt with wingtip or lay-down collar
◇ Black shirt studs

MICHAEL NOLTE'S
WEDDING PLANNING CHECKLIST

"How To" for "I Do"

TO DO IMMEDIATELY

◇ Establish your budget
◇ Alphabetize a master guest list
◇ Reserve ceremony location
◇ Reserve reception site
◇ Contact officiate
◇ Hire photographer
◇ Hire band or DJ
◇ Contract florist
◇ Contract caterer
◇ Contract videographer
◇ Contract organist
◇ Contract vocalist
◇ Contract other musicians

◇ Contract limo
◇ Contract for hair and makeup
◇ Contract for wedding cake
◇ Announce engagement in newspaper
◇ Reserve rehearsal dinner site
◇ Reserve rental equipment
◇ Reserve hotel rooms
◇ Register for gifts

SHOPPING LIST FOR THE BRIDE

◇ Gown
◇ Headpiece
◇ Jewelry
◇ Shoes

- ◇ Gloves
- ◇ Garter
- ◇ Gown preservation
- ◇ Seamstress

SHOPPING LIST FOR THE BRIDESMAIDS

- ◇ Gown
- ◇ Jewelry
- ◇ Shoes
- ◇ Gloves
- ◇ Gifts
- ◇ Seamstress

SHOPPING LIST FOR THE MOTHERS

- ◇ Dresses
- ◇ Shoes
- ◇ Jewelry
- ◇ Purses
- ◇ Seamstress

SHOPPING LIST FOR THE MEN

- ◇ Tuxedos

APPOINTMENTS TO MAKE

- ◇ Portrait sitting
- ◇ Marriage license
- ◇ Pre-wedding conference with clergy
- ◇ Hair, makeup, and manicures for bridal party

SELECTIONS TO MAKE

- ◇ Rehearsal dinner menu
- ◇ Reception menu
- ◇ Music for ceremony
- ◇ Reception music

GENERAL TO-DO

- ◇ Arrange lodging for attendants
- ◇ Develop guest lists for showers
- ◇ Open joint checking account
- ◇ Change name on driver's license
- ◇ Change name on social security card
- ◇ List fiancé as life insurance beneficiary
- ◇ Make honeymoon reservations
- ◇ Write place cards for rehearsal and reception
- ◇ Select or make attendants' gifts
- ◇ Prepare payment envelopes for organist, minister, etc.
- ◇ Arrange transportation from church to reception for bridal party
- ◇ Assign someone to transfer gifts from reception
- ◇ Arrange for babysitter for out-of-town children
- ◇ Delegate someone to coordinate out-of-towners' arrivals and pickups
- ◇ Appoint someone to return the tuxes
- ◇ Submit newspaper announcement

CHAPTER TWO

Embellishments!

In keeping with her goal to host a wedding that was light, fresh, and understated, Kelly chose a simple dress and elbow-length veil. It was the perfect decision for an August wedding.

Let's Get Started

In the months leading up to Kelly's wedding, we began to refer to our home as Wedding Central One and Kelly's apartment as Wedding Central Two. The phone lines between our two command centers hummed as we tackled each delightful detail of her upcoming celebration.

From the very beginning, I left all the big questions up to Kelly because I felt it was essential that she have control over every aspect of her big day. Kelly has impeccable taste, so I couldn't wait to see what she came up with.

❦ Attending to Attire ❦

Kelly wanted a simple, timeless dress that worked well for a home wedding and garden reception. After a few shopping excursions, she found a beautiful strapless A-line gown that looked beautiful on her. The only problem was, the dress sported a long train and puffy tulle underskirt—two features Kelly knew she absolutely didn't want.

She went back several times to try on the dress, and the last time, asked me to come along to give my opinion. I knew once I saw the dress on her that it was the one. It just needed a few tweaks to fit her needs, so the bridal boutique trimmed the train and took out the clouds of tulle. Every minute spent agonizing over the dress was worth it when we saw Britt's face light up as he caught sight of his beautiful bride descending the steps toward him.

With the bridal gown decided, Kelly turned her attention to her bridesmaids' dresses. She knew she wanted her maids dressed in her favorite color, green, so she selected darling off-the-shoulder cocktail-length dresses in a sublime light green chiffon. Because Kelly wanted her wedding to feel more like a dinner party, she opted for the groom and his groomsmen to wear formal black suits, not tuxedos. For Britt, she selected a white tie that matched her gown.

Britt's parents and Dan and I all dressed in black evening attire, with the men in black suits, and Markie and me in black dresses.

❧ Finding a Photographer ❧

Kelly wanted to find a photographer who was as relaxed and informal as she wanted her wedding to be. She interviewed one photographer whose work was beautiful, but he was so jittery, she knew he would make her nervous during the wedding. She tossed his card and moved on. Finally she zeroed in on a photographer whose candid, photojournalistic approach to wedding photography captured the fluid look she wanted. Once she saw that his laid-back personality would make him fun to work with, the deal was sealed.

For us, selecting a caterer was the easiest decision of them all. We simply got on our knees and pleaded with our dear friend Cheryl Hartell to create her culinary magic for our guests. A professional chef who owns a fine-dining restaurant near our home, Cheryl has spoiled us by making masterful meals for nearly every event we hold in our home. We knew whatever she prepared would be fabulous, so we left the entire menu selection up to her, a luxury I know most brides don't have with their caterers. With Cheryl on our team, the guests would go home with full stomachs and big smiles.

As a lover of great food, I firmly believe any memorable event must include a spread of fabulous fare. For that reason, it's essential that you find a skilled chef to cater your wedding celebration and then choose your menu with great care.

TIPS FROM THE EXPERTS

TANTALIZING CUISINE

Advice from Cheryl Hartell,
gourmet chef and owner of The Vineyards Restaurant in Weston, Missouri

❧ LOOK FOR A CATERER WHO PREPARES FOOD THAT'S OUT OF THE ORDINARY. Dare to go beyond meatballs! A wedding reception is the perfect opportunity to sample new and unusual foods. Try a few dishes with international flair or ethnic cuisine that honors the heritage of the bride and groom.

❧ MAKE SURE THE CATERER USES FRESH, LOCALLY GROWN AND SEASONALLY APPROPRIATE INGREDIENTS. Cheryl is passionate about using only the finest ingredients when she cooks and suggests that the chef who prepares the dishes for your wedding should be, too. You can't beat the taste of just-plucked fruits and veggies, so don't settle for anything less.

❧ ASK FOR REFERENCES. Get a list of people who have used the caterer in the past few months, and then ask each one a host of questions about the quality of the food and the professionalism of the service.

☙ Ask for a tasting. Before you sign the contract, see for yourself if the caterer is as good as everyone says. Pick a few items from the menu that you'd like to serve. Or, ask the chef to suggest something unusual. Be sure to offer to pay for food costs.

☙ Be up front with your budget and needs. If your event is too small or too large for the caterer, it's best to know that right up front so you can continue your search.

☙ Look for chemistry. To preserve your sanity, work only with a caterer who is a good listener, accommodating to your needs, and easy to get along with.

☙ Look for experience. How long has the caterer been preparing food for weddings? Will your reception be one of several events the caterer works that day or will you have the chef's undivided attention? Has the caterer ever worked at the venue where your reception will be held?

☙ Find someone who will work around your party's special needs. If you have guests with food allergies or dietary concerns, it's important your caterer be willing to provide menu items that meet their needs.

☙ Request they use only professional servers. You want an attentive and cheerful wait staff that is quick to refresh drinks and clear away dishes.

☙ Remember the kids. If your party includes little ones, see if the caterer will provide a few kid-friendly foods.

A MENU OF DINING OPTIONS

FORMAL DINNER.

A formal banquet is, without a doubt, the height of wedding elegance. If you want to treat guests to this wonderful dining experience, select a reception venue with a kitchen and food prep area large enough to prepare and plate the food. You'll also need a large serving staff to attend to guests' needs. When choosing your menu, Cheryl recommends offering guests a choice of seafood, poultry, beef, and vegetarian entrées.

BUFFET.

Preparing a beautiful buffet is a perfect option for those who want to treat their guests to a marvelous meal without the formality, complication, or expense of a sit-down dinner. Be sure your buffet selections offer a variety of appetizers, side dishes, and entrées.

HORS D'OEUVRES.

If your reception will be held before or after customary mealtimes, you can serve a selection of hot and cold hors d'oeuvres. As a courtesy, Cheryl advises letting guests know ahead of time that a light offering of hors d'oeuvres will be served so they know to eat before the ceremony. She also recommends picking hors d'oeuvres that are finger- or fork-friendly so guests can enjoy them as they mill about the reception.

DELIGHTFUL DESSERTS.

If you're on a budget, Cheryl suggests selecting a lower-cost but fun theme for your reception, like a dessert bar loaded with tantalizing sweet treats, from small cakes and tarts to chocolate fondue.

CHOOSING A COLOR PALETTE

Since Kelly's wedding would be held outdoors during the scorching month of August, she knew she needed to pick a light and cool color scheme. Green, her favorite color, was a natural. And when she paired it with pink, it evoked images of soft spring afternoons.

My friend Melanie Krumbholz's daughter, Amber Schreiber, followed a very different trail to find her beautiful color palette. Amber didn't have any particular color scheme in mind, but when she fell in love with a latte-colored bridal gown, her color scheme became crystal clear. I think these colors are perfect choices anytime of the year. On the following spread, I've picked some fabrics that also work well with these earthier tones, including a brown velvet swatch that would be perfect for a winter wedding.

Bride: Amber Krumbholz Schreiber

Latte, Cream, and Chocolate

Amber was uncertain about the latte-colored dress when she paired it with the bridesmaid's gowns. But when she held it up against the dresses of chocolate brown, both looked so yummy, she knew she'd found the perfect combination. I love how Amber mixed her palette of latte, cream, and chocolate into every facet of her wedding celebration, from the invitations to the bows on the guests' party favors. This trio of tones drenched every detail of her wedding in a warm, rich glow, including the neutral colors of her floral centerpieces at the wedding.

Mr. and Mrs. David Krumholtz
REQUEST THE HONOUR OF YOUR PRESENCE
AT THE MARRIAGE OF THEIR DAUGHTER

Amber Elizabeth
TO

Burt David Schreiber
SON OF

Mr. and Mrs. Dennis Schreiber

SATURDAY, THE TWELFTH OF AUGUST
TWO THOUSAND AND SIX
AT SIX O'CLOCK IN THE EVENING

OUR LADY OF SORROWS
2552 GILLHAM ROAD
KANSAS CITY, MISSOURI

PHOTOS BY ISAAC ALONGI

EMBELLISHMENTS! ✨ 51

PICKING FLOWERS

When Kelly started thinking about the personal bouquets and decorative floral arrangements we would use in her wedding, she wasn't exactly sure what she wanted. However, she was clear on what she didn't want: roses.

One day, as Kelly flipped through wedding magazines tearing out pictures of floral arrangements she loved, she handed me a photo of a beautiful bouquet. "What are these flowers?" She asked. "They're roses," I laughed. She was an instant convert and made sure every floral we had included roses.

Kelly and I both love flowers so much that we had to rein ourselves in to keep from using so many bouquets there would be no room for people in the house. In addition to a few grand bouquets in the foyer, we incorporated fresh flower arrangements into the table centerpieces and buffet. Petite silver trays of appetizers also featured simple nosegays. And the party favors were silver mint julep cups cradling mini bouquets.

TIPS FROM THE EXPERTS

FABULOUS FLOWERS

Advice from Kelly Acock,
owner of and floral artist for Monarch Flower Company

When I first saw Kelly Acock's work I was captivated by her innovative approach to decorating with flowers, her unbridled enthusiasm, and her careful attention to her brides' wishes. I asked her to share advice on how other brides could ensure their wedding flowers would be fabulous too. A large part of your overall budget for the wedding might be spent on flowers, so it's imperative that you find the right person for you. Here's what she recommends.

1 FIND THE FLORIST WHO IS RIGHT FOR YOU.

⚘ START EARLY. Many florists book up early for popular dates. If you have your heart set on a particular florist who is in high demand, you may need to get on his or her schedule up to a year and a half in advance.

⚘ ASK AROUND. Recent brides, wedding coordinators, and other industry professionals can usually recommend florists who do fabulous work.

⚘ INTERVIEW THREE FLORISTS. Don't just go with the first name you get.

⚘ SEE WHAT THE FLORIST IS DOING. Peek in on a wedding the florist is decorating.

⚘ SEE IF THE FLORIST HAS SUPPLIES YOU CAN RENT. Rent items like vases, so you don't have to purchase them yourself.

⚘ ASK THE FLORIST HOW HE OR SHE WOULD BRING YOUR WEDDING THEME OR COLOR PALETTE TO LIFE. You want someone who is enthusiastic and full of creative ideas.

⚘ INQUIRE WHAT HE OR SHE CAN DO FOR YOUR BUDGET. You want to work only with someone who is comfortable with the amount you are able to invest.

2 | PREPARE FOR YOUR FIRST MEETING.

❧ PICK YOUR COLOR PALETTE OR THEME. If you're having trouble zeroing in on a cohesive look for the wedding, start with your favorite color. If the bride and groom met at a beach, perhaps seashells could be the wedding's theme. Or you could center your color palette on the colors and bounty of the season.

❧ COLLECT PHOTOS OF SEVERAL FLORAL ARRANGEMENTS. Choose arrangements you love and those you hate to give the florist a good feel for your taste.

❧ TAKE PHOTOS. Take pictures of your wedding gown and the ceremony and reception venues.

❧ KNOW WHAT'S HOT. The flowers brides can't get enough of today include cymbidium orchids, hydrangeas, and roses. Right now, brides are clamoring for anything limey green, like Jade and Super Green roses, trachilium, hanging amaranthus, bells of Ireland, hypericum berries, and bupleurum.

3 | DECIDE WHERE YOU'LL USE FLOWERS.

❧ PERSONAL FLOWERS. Your florist should have a checklist that details who in your wedding party should have personal flowers. Personal flowers can be done in a myriad of ways, so have fun looking through your florist's idea books until you find the tone and look that makes your heart skip a beat.

🌿 CEREMONY FLOWERS. Plan one stop-them-in-their-tracks arrangement in the most visible location, such as the entry to the ceremony site, on the altar, or in another spot where the bride and groom will take their vows. Kelly also loves to put petite arrangements along the center aisle, affixing them to the outside of every third row of seats.

🌿 RECEPTION FLOWERS. By all means, use flowers to dress up your cake table, head table, buffet, dining tables, gift table, on the bar, and in the ladies' room. For added drama, consider decorating the chandeliers with floral garlands or suspend a wreath of flowers above each dining table.

H DOUBLE THE PLEASURE BY REUSING FLORAL ARRANGEMENTS.

Instead of having separate flowers for the wedding and reception, you can use the same flowers for each. The secret is to present the flowers in completely different ways at the wedding and reception so guests never guess they are the same.

🌿 AISLE FLOWERS. Reuse the flowers that decorated the center aisle as reception centerpieces. For instance, if you used floral wreaths to brighten the center aisle, for the reception, lay them flat at the center of the dining tables and fill them with pillar candles.

🌿 GRAND BOUQUET. Snatch the bouquet from the altar, disassemble it, and use the flowers in several smaller arrangements on the head table or cake table.

≈ ENTRANCE FLOWERS. Cluster a beautiful group of potted plants and flowers in a basket at the entrance to the ceremony venue, and then remove the individual pots and put them on each dining table.

≈ BRIDESMAIDS' BOUQUETS. Insert bridesmaids' bouquets in waiting vases on the cake table or along a buffet table.

5 | TRY TODAY'S HOTTEST FLORAL CENTERPIECE TRENDS.

≈ GET FRUITY. Fruits and vegetables like lemons, limes, sliced apples, cranberries, pomegranates, grapes, artichokes, asparagus, broccoli, and cauliflower are being invited to the table to create knockout arrangements loaded with color and texture.

≈ TRY A BREAKAWAY DESIGN. Find a vase design that comes in three different sizes and select three kinds of flowers that offer diverse textures and colors. Then make mounded, single-stem bouquets in each vase, clustering the trio together atop a silver riser or elegant cake plate. If you want a lofty look, opt for tall cylinders or fluted vases.

≈ LIGHT THE FIRE. Candles have added spark to centerpieces for years. Now they're taking center stage. Fill the center of a long

banquet table with a phalanx of different-size cylinder candles. Or create a blocked grid of votives, breaking up the geometric pattern with a row of votive holders filled with flowers.

≈ TAKE THE PLUNGE. Submerged flowers are all the rage today. Wind flexible-stemmed flowers at the bottom of clear cylinder vases filled with water, add a second layer of flowers or petals, and top with a floating candle.

≈ REACH FOR THE SKY. For dramatic height, fill a tall cylinder with flowering tree branches.

≈ GO LIVE. Pot rustic plants like hens and chicks or moss in silver mint julep cups, and then cluster them in the center of the table.

KELLY
GARRITY   **&**   BRITT
BIERI

Together with their parents
request the pleasure of your company
at their wedding
Saturday, the nineteenth of August
two thousand and six
at half after seven o'clock in the evening
at the home of
Mr and Mrs Dan Garrity
420 North Third Street
Atchison, Kansas

Courtyard reception to follow

*Kelly and her attendants
prepared for the wedding in
the guest room, where I put
out champagne flutes and
enlisted the help of this rustic statue to elevate the tone
to new heights.*

Details

DECORATIONS

When Kelly was ready to tackle the decorations for her big day, I was bursting with ideas. She wanted the decorations to be light, fresh, and romantic, but most of all, understated. I'm wild about silver, so I had to add plenty of sparkle and pop with gorgeous candlesticks and scads of beautiful silver trays. But the decorative element that made Kelly's wedding simply magical was the dramatic lighting inside and out. From the candle-covered wreaths hanging from the towering trees in our front yard to the dramatic thirteen-armed candelabra in the reception tent, everywhere you turned, candles glowed in the soft August dusk.

INVITATIONS

At first, Kelly thought about working with Britt's sister Kirsten to create her own invitations. But as she looked over supplies for homemade cards, she realized that wasn't what she wanted at all. Instead, she opted to order invitations from a shop. It didn't take Kelly long to zero in on a simple yet stylish invitation in off-white and green.

TIPS FROM THE EXPERTS

THE ABCs OF INVITATIONS

Advice from Abby Albers,
proprietor of RSVP, a store that specializes
in printed materials for special events

> KELLY
> GARRITY   &   BRITT
>   BIERI
>
> Together with their parents
> request the pleasure of your company
> at their wedding
> Saturday, the nineteenth of August
> two thousand and six
> at half after seven o'clock in the evening
> at the home of
> Mr. and Mrs. Dan Garrity
> 420 North Third Street
> Atchison, Kansas
>
> Courtyard reception to follow

Your invitations will set the tone for your entire wedding, giving guests a glimpse of what's in store. So assemble an invitation packet that reflects the look and feel of your wedding. I asked invitation pro Abby Albers, who often creates invitations for my parties, to offer her advice on how to pick wedding invitations you'll love:

STEP ONE: Decide what style of invitation best suits your event. Invitations have come a long way since yesteryear, when your choices were limited to white or ecru. Now you can pick from a dizzying array of colors, a wide assortment of papers, and some unusual and even funky formats.

STEP TWO: Consider the printing process you want to use.

Engraving. In this process, considered the most elite form of printing, a metal die is cut and used to engrave a pattern, which is then filled in with ink, to create a distinctive raised-letter look.

Thermography. This popular printing technique closely mimics the raised-letter appearance of engraved printing but for a fraction of the cost.

Letterpress. Similar to engraving, letterpress printing also uses a metal plate, but the image is pressed on the top of the paper, not the bottom, so the letters recede into the paper.

Flat printing. The lowest-cost alternative, flat printing is used on almost all normal printed pieces.

⁓ STEP THREE: Pick the components of your invitation packet. Most wedding invitation packets include an invitation to the wedding ceremony, an invitation to the reception, and a response card and envelope that guests use to RSVP.

Traditionally, wedding invitations were sent in two carrier envelopes, with the outside bearing the guests' address and the inside simply inscribed with the guests' names. Abby says roughly half of the brides she works with use double envelopes because they like the formal approach and half use single carrier envelopes because they don't want the added work of inscribing and stuffing a second envelope.

Sometimes brides add additional pieces to their invitation packet, such as accommodation cards with information on hotels for out-of-town guests, maps to the reception, "within the ribbon" cards for VIP guests who are invited to sit at the front of the ceremony, and invitations to other wedding-related events.

⁓ STEP FOUR: Leave yourself plenty of time to address and mail your invitations. Abby suggests ordering your invitation packet so it comes in at least two months before your wedding date, giving you a month to address the invitations and get them in the mail a month prior to the ceremony.

OTHER PRINTED PIECES YOU MIGHT NEED

SAVE-THE-DATE CARDS.
⁓ It's a good idea to let your guests know up to a year ahead when your wedding will be, especially if they will need to make flight arrangements.

PROGRAMS.
⁓ Your ceremony program can do so much more than simply list the order of events. You can fill it with thank-you sentiments, at-home information, and even brief bios on each member of the wedding party.

THANK-YOU NOTES.
⁓ Order thank-you notes that coordinate with your wedding invitations, so your printed pieces have a uniform look.

AT-HOME CARDS.
⁓ These helpful notes give the newlyweds' new contact information.

RECEPTION PIECES.
⁓ These include table menus, place cards, table assignments, and cocktail napkins.

CHAPTER THREE
Celebrations!

Showers of Love

When it came to bridal showers, Kelly had the best of both worlds. Some dear friends of our family threw her a "girly-girl" brunch that made her feel like a princess. And at an outdoor barbecue hosted by friends of Britt's family, she got to meet folks who'd known her future husband all his life.

PRETTY IN PINK

When Kelly and I walked into our friend Mary Sullivan's home and saw the enchanting party she and her sister, Denise Janes, and sister-in-law, Janet Seeman, prepared for us, we squealed with delight. These amazing women, who are really more like family than friends, never do things partway. Even though we had set our sights high, we were still amazed by the amount of love they poured into even the tiniest details.

Before these talented sisters planned the party, they wisely asked Kelly what type of shower she wanted. Kelly surprised us all by saying that instead of a themed shower, she wanted a casual but elegant

luncheon that allowed the women to mix and mingle.

Without a theme to inspire the decorations, our able hostesses took their cues from the wedding palette of pink and green. They wove touches of the color scheme into nearly every detail of the event, from the invitations to the magnificent dining tables to the party favors.

After being greeted at the door with a mimosa drink, the guests mingled throughout the house, which was dressed up with bouquets of hydrangea blossoms and hosta leaves, snipped fresh from Mary's garden. To create continuity in their party decorations, they used similar bouquets on the mantel, buffet, dining tables, and cake table.

The highlight of the light luncheon was the chicken salad, a sentimental family recipe Mary's grandmother-in-law served at the bridal shower she'd hosted for Mary. For dessert, the sisters surprised us with a custom cake that looked like a stack of gifts wrapped in pink and green paper.

In order to seat all the guests comfortably, they rented round tables and ballroom chairs and set them up throughout the house. Then they dressed them festively with pops of pink and green, like iridescent pink dessert plates and reversible pink and green napkins. Next to our places, we found a fabulous party favor: a pink and green kitchen towel and potholder.

SECRETS FOR SUCCESSFUL BRIDAL EVENTS

~ MAKE SURE THE EVENT REFLECTS THE PERSONALITY OF THE BRIDE. If the bride loves to be the life of the party, throw a large gathering with guys and gals. But if she's shy, she might prefer a small luncheon with just a few close friends.

~ ASK THE BRIDE FOR HER PREFERENCES. Does she want a themed shower or not? Is she crazy about party games or do party games make her crazy? Remember, this event is about her, so plan everything around her likes and dislikes.

~ TEAM UP WITH FRIENDS. Throwing bridal events can take a lot of time and financial resources, so ask a few friends to host with you. If you prefer to go it alone, make sure you have help the day of the party with cooking, serving, and cleaning up so you can enjoy the party, too.

~ BE ORGANIZED. As with any entertaining, the more organized you are ahead of time, the better the event will come off. Decorate several days before the party so you aren't rushing around minutes before guests arrive.

~ PICK OUT PERFECT INVITATIONS. Invitations set the tone for the entire event, so pick out a style that lets guests know whether this will be a formal, casual, or festive gathering.

~ INCORPORATE THE WEDDING'S PALETTE AND THEME. Weave these elements into every aspect of your event, from your invitations to your decorations.

~ MAKE YOUR TABLETOP A VISUAL FEAST. Whether you're hosting a light luncheon for the bridesmaids or a dinner party for the bride and groom's parents, make your dining table as beautiful, romantic, and memorable as the occasion. Set the tone with a dramatic centerpiece, such as a bouquet of fresh flowers that match those that will be used in the wedding.

~ SPOIL GUESTS WITH PARTY FAVORS. To commemorate the event, give guests small keepsakes that will remind them of the bride.

Let's Get the Party Started

I am certifiably crazy about parties. I love to host them, I live to attend them, and I even imagine being there when people describe parties *they've* hosted or attended. It's no wonder I'm nuts about weddings, because what is a wedding if not a big party?

For a party girl like me, the months of festivities that lead up to the Big Day are Nirvana. Best yet, I've found that the celebrations that surround weddings are second to none. The joy of the event seems to inspire hostesses to new heights of creativity. When I attend engagement dinners, bridal showers, bridesmaids' luncheons, rehearsal dinners, and wedding receptions, I am constantly wowed by their inventive themes, amazing decorations, fabulous food, and memorable party gifts.

As I drink in every detail, I leave brimming with enthusiasm and full of ideas for my next gathering. I hope you'll feel the same way, as some of my creative friends and experienced wedding experts share how to make your wedding parties second to none.

≈ Shower Themes ≈

I love themed showers because I think it's exciting to bring creative ideas to life through invitations, decorations, and parting gifts for guests. The sky's the limit when it comes to shower themes, so ask the bride for ideas, suggest your own, or choose one of the following popular categories: tools and garage, barbecue, stock the bar, around the clock, kitchen, garden, honeymoon, lingerie, linens , home accents, entertainment.

"BIERI" SPECIAL EVENT

On Britt's side of the family, a group of old friends threw a couple's barbecue shower for Kelly and Britt. The centerpiece for this festive event featured colorful strawberry plants.

For this casual outdoor affair, the hosts dressed up their deck with tables covered in red-and-white gingham tablecloths and served barbecue catered by a local restaurant, a hint at the fabulous gift the group purchased for the bride and groom.

Prior to the party, the hosts asked party guests to go in on a barbecue grill instead of purchasing individual gifts for the bride and groom. Between them, they were able to purchase a grill that Kelly swears is bigger than their car.

Best yet, the barbecue shower proved to be the perfect setting for Kelly to get to know many of Britt's family's dearest friends, many of whom had known Britt since he was a baby.

Keep the Party Fresh

I am always amazed by the clever details that friends and family have shared with me over the years and how they implement their bride's interests in their party plans. This clever shower actually started on the front porch at the entrance to this charming cottage. The hostess set an arrangement of fresh edible herbs out between her porch chairs to greet arriving guests. Along the rail she set individual glass herb pots festooned with ribbons so that as the guests left the party, they received a parting gift from the hostess.

Rather than a shower, another friend of mine put all of her pre-wedding energy into hosting an engagement party for her brother and sister-in-law-to-be six months before the wedding. She invited only the immediate families of the bride and groom, their spouses, and children, so that everyone could meet and get to know each other before the bigger demands of the wedding took over their lives. She used the bride's color palette to set the mood, and even though it was winter outside, inside she captured the excitement of the coming spring event.

One dear friend put together an incredibly clever and intimate luncheon for her new daughter-in-law-to-be the day of the rehearsal dinner and invited only her bridal party. This small gathering gave everyone time to relax before the big day and gave the bride some quality time to really visit with her best friends before the big weekend began.

❧ Superlative Decorations ❧

When Dan and I watch movies, he teases me that I'm the only person he knows who is more interested in the interiors shown in the film than in the plot. As our family contracted wedding fever, my passion shifted to *Father of the Bride.* I'm crazy about the wedding decor in both the old version and the remake because of its opulent, classic style.

At the risk of sounding overly simple, the decorations for any bridal celebration, whether it be an engagement party, a bridal luncheon, a rehearsal dinner, or a wedding reception, need to be drop-dead gorgeous. They are the secret to bringing the color palette and theme to life and making the chosen venue shine.

Here are a few of my favorite decorating tips you can tailor to make any event you host for the bride and groom luscious and lovely.

LIGHTING

Like any woman of a certain age, I am a pushover for soft, forgiving, romantic candlelight. And whenever I entertain, I use truckloads of tapers, votives, and tea lights. In fact, when it's time to blow out the candles at the

end of an event, I send up such a cloud of smoke, I'm surprised the neighbors don't call the fire department.

But in recent years, I've switched my allegiance from traditional candles to those that are battery operated. Today's faux candles offer all the beauty of the real things, but with none of the hassles or danger. For instance, you can turn on battery-operated candles hours before your event, saving yourself the last-minute panic of lighting all the candles just before guests arrive. They don't blow out or drip wax. And at the end of the evening, you can leave them glowing without risking a fire hazard.

Perhaps I'm so passionate about lighting because it's one of the most effective ways to add surprise and drama to your events. When I hosted my niece Becca's garden wedding reception, we had to rent portable bathrooms to accommodate the large number of guests. Determined to not let these eyesores spoil the look of the reception, I decided to decorate them to the nines with some unexpected lighting. In addition to covering the interior walls with scrim and adding linen hand towels, I fitted each potty with a petite crystal chandelier. Guests were so shocked and amazed by the latrines, they had their pictures taken in them!

When adding dramatic lighting to your events, first focus on the background light. If your event will be held outdoors, consider hanging candelabras or votive cups from trees and bushes. If you're having an event in a hall with drop ceilings, use hooks to suspend crystal chandeliers or wreath candelabras over each dining table.

Then turn your attention to filling each dining table with soft light. Use ornate silver candelabra, rustic lanterns filled with candles and flowers, or a medley of pillar candles and votives marching down the middle of the table.

Get creative as you survey your venue. How else can you brighten the spot with unexpected or unusual lighting? I worked with a bride who placed large glass cylinders at the center of each dining table, filled them with fallen branches she'd misted silver and gold, and then hung votive tea lights from the twigs.

CENTERPIECES

Centerpieces steal the show at every event, and they should at your wedding celebration, too. Whether you create displays on the dining tables, the gift table, or the buffet, make sure they make guests' jaws drop.

The secret to building a memorable centerpiece is to add loads of drama. I like to do this by working with a mix of beautiful pieces of different heights, textures, and tones.

When creating your centerpieces, be sure they are in keeping with the venue. I recently attended a casual country wedding with a picnic reception. Each table was dotted with a row of wildflower bouquets in Mason jars. Simple and clean, this casual, edited look was perfect for the event.

Instead of using the same centerpiece treatment on each table at a wedding reception, I'm a big fan of mixing it up. I love to use three different-size treatments that share a common theme, color, or decorative piece so the centerpieces look harmonious, not chaotic, when grouped together.

My friend Kathy Fernholz pulled this off beautifully at her daughter, Katie's, wedding. To accent Katie's color palette of black and cream, Kathy created three centerpiece treatments, each sporting a black container holding floral arrangements that included not just flowers, but artichokes, limes, pears, and grapes. For the smallest centerpiece, she filled a black iron basket with flowers. For the medium display, she placed flowers in a black iron urn. And the tall centerpiece sported flowers atop a candlestick embellished with prisms reclaimed from an old lamp that belonged to Katie's great-grandmother.

TABLE LINENS

There is so much you can do with wedding table linens these days. Sometimes I keep my linens classic and quiet so the table setting can steal the show. Other times, I like to energize a table with linens full of pattern and color.

If you're seating a large party, consider acquiring linens from an event rental company. Many companies have a wonderful assortment of classic to funky tablecloths and napkins. Or make your own custom linens, like Kathy did for Katie's wedding. A professional home decor seamstress, Kathy designed three different tablecloths for the tables at Katie's reception, each in complementary black and cream toile, buffalo check, and stripe. After the wedding, Kathy reclaimed the tablecloths and used the fabric in the new bedding ensemble she made for her bedroom.

CREATIVE COLOR PALETTES

Bride: Katie Fernholz Pandullo

Black and Cream

Katie did an amazing job of making wedding magic with one of my very favorite color palettes. She and her mom, Kathy Fernholz, made tablecloths from three complementary black and cream fabrics—toile, a bold floral, diamond-patterned weave, and buffalo check—to dress up the head table and thirty round dining tables. Her choice of coordinating fabrics made the large room more intimate and personal. In fact, Katie brought a personal touch into nearly every aspect of her wedding celebration, whether it was using her grandmother's horseshoe pin in her bouquet or her new monogram on her dinner napkins.

TABLE SETTINGS

I'm a fanatic about dishes and love to create tabletops that feel like works of art. In my opinion, there's no better time to put on the ritz than at a wedding celebration, so by all means, do your table up big, with fine china, crystal, and silver.

When you dress your table for any bridal event, be sure to work the wedding color palette and theme into everything from your centerpiece to your linens to your napkin rings. If your reception venue provides the dishware and stemware, consider adding a custom spark with a personal salad plate, party favor, or name card.

PLACE CARDS

Creative place cards are a fun and easy way to make each guest feel welcomed. Inscribe guests' names onto cards, and then tuck them into a tiny vase filled with flowers, tie them to a beautifully wrapped party favor box, or insert them into a groove cut in a piece of seasonal fruit.

MENU CARDS

I think the addition of beautiful menu cards displayed before each dish on a buffet or at each guest's place at dinner instantly elevates a simple meal to a fine event. Stand the menu card in an unusual holder or on an easel. Or tuck it into a pocket created in a dinner napkin placed atop the dishes.

CHAIR BACKS

Your table will be all the more irresistible when you decorate the backs of the dining chairs. Cover them with yards of romantic fabric tied up with decorative ribbon. If you're having a small gathering, hang a floral wreath or a basket of flowers from each chair back. If it's a large crowd, simply dress up the chairs of the guests of honor.

When I entertain on a grand scale, I almost always turn to my favorite event rental company for help. I'm sold on renting equipment, dishes, and linens for big events because it's both a cost- and time-efficient way to entertain. For Kelly's wedding, we rented everything from the tent to the tablecloths. If you've never rented supplies for a party, you might be amazed by the array of party pieces most event rental companies carry:

EQUIPMENT
Tents
Stages
Dance floors
Ballroom chairs
Fans and heaters
Turf
Picket fences
Red carpet runner

LINENS
Tablecloths
Table overlays
Napkins

TABLEWARE
China dishes
Silver and stainless flatware
Stemware
Silver trays
Coffee urns
Champagne fountains

DECORATIONS
Themed decor for special events
Candlesticks
Urns

One of the great pleasures
of planning a wedding is the
way we choose to personal-
ize it. All of the little details
that make each aspect of the
celebration special come together to create a memorable
event. Gifts for the bride, as
well as for the attendants,
are an important part of the
planning process.

Gifts Galore

Have fun coming up with unique gifts that will let your wedding party know how much they mean to you. Some brides thank their bridesmaids by paying for their dresses, jewelry, and shoes. Others present them with a beautiful token, like a crystal perfume decanter or jewelry box. Still others lovingly craft gifts from scratch, like Kathy did for Katie's wedding party.

A wiz on the sewing machine, Kathy stitched and monogrammed black and cream canvas totes for each of Katie's six bridesmaids. She also made zippered cosmetic bags and jewelry bags out of complementary black and cream fabrics and tucked them inside the totes. For fun, she even decorated flip-flop shoes for the bridesmaids to wear during the reception if their feet got tired.

To Welcome Out-of-Town Guests

Since a number of guests for her daughter, Amber's, wedding were traveling from out of town, my friend Melanie wanted to greet them in style, so she created the most adorable welcome gifts I've ever seen. She filled silver ice buckets with brochures on the local sites, area maps, and historic information about the venues for the wedding and reception. She also inserted a booklet she created that listed the times and locations of each wedding event and everyone in the bridal party's mobile phone numbers. She then filled the space remaining in the ice bucket with tasty treats purchased from the city's signature eateries, like gourmet popcorn and specialty cookies.

To Thank Wedding Guests

Since I'm still a kid at heart, I love to receive party favors when I attend events. It's a fun surprise to see what the hostess selects, and the gifts always serve as wonderful keepsakes to commemorate the time you've spent together. Here are a few ways to thank those who have shared this day of celebration with you:

- CD OF THE NEWLYWEDS' FAVORITE ROMANTIC TUNES. Fill a disk and make a label with songs played during the wedding ceremony and reception or the couple's favorite love songs.

- CANDY BUFFET. Let guests indulge their sweet tooth as they make their own yummy treat bags to take home. Fill apothecary jars with a wide variety of candies. Lay out a silver scoop and small bags and let guests help themselves.

✑ BLOOMING MEMORIES. Give guests packets of flower seeds or a wrapped bulb to plant so they can think of the bride and groom every time they enjoy their garden, or fill a tiny galvanized bucket or terra-cotta pot with forced bulbs like grape hyacinths.

✑ BOXES OF BITE-SIZE TREATS. The sky's the limit when it comes to decorating and filling petite boxes with edible treats. Purchase decorative boxes or have fun creating your own with ribbons, lace, and flowers. Inside, tuck in anything from truffles to iced sugar cookies bearing the bride and groom's monogram.

✑ SWEET-SMELLING SOMETHING. Fill mini boxes or decorative bags with scented soap, potpourri, or perfumed candles.

✑ VOTIVES. Embellish plain votive holders to match the color or theme of your wedding.

✑ APERITIFS. Tie a bow around small bottles of liqueur. For fun, switch out the bottle's original label and replace it with one bearing the happy couple's picture and wedding date.

✑ DONATIONS TO CHARITY. Instead of giving party favors to guests, Amber and Burt Schreiber donated the amount they would have spent on favors to their favorite charity in their guests' names. However, mother of the bride Melanie didn't want guests to leave empty handed, so she sent them on their way with a freshly baked cookie in a decorative bag affixed with the newlyweds' at-home information.

PHOTOS BY ISAAC ALONGI

Bride: Kate Ackerman Jones

Tiffany Blue and White

When Kate chose the timeless color of Tiffany blue for her wedding, she set a regal tone for the entire event. Her reception was held in a grand ballroom, where 350 guests enjoyed a formal sit-down dinner. With the help of wedding coordinator Michael Nolte, Kate artfully combined bold color accents and soft lighting to create a magical evening loaded with drama. The two-tone color palette is clean and dramatic. Here are some fabric choices to go along with this color choice, but are all a bit casual and textured and would set a more informal mood.

TIPS FROM THE EXPERTS

THE VOICE OF EXPERIENCE

Michael Nolte shares how a bride can make her wedding day dramatic

❧ TRUST YOUR PROFESSIONALS. Give them your vote of confidence, and then stay out of their way.

❧ LET YOUR WEDDING GOWN BE A SURPRISE TO ALL. Don't show your dress to anyone other than the person who is paying for it, the florist, and the seamstress. Don't describe it to friends or try it on more than twice.

❧ DON'T VIEW THE DECORATED WEDDING VENUE BEFORE THE CEREMONY. Drink it in for the first time as you walk down the aisle.

❧ DON'T LET THE GROOM SEE YOU BEFORE THE WEDDING. Let him anticipate the magical moment when you enter in your wedding gown.

❧ KEEP THE WEDDING DRESSING ROOM PRIVATE. The dressing area should be open to the wedding party only.

❧ DO NOT ALLOW THE POST-CEREMONY PHOTO SHOOT TO LAST LONGER THAN TWENTY MINUTES. It's time to greet guests at the celebration!

~ WEAR YOUR VEIL EVERY MINUTE YOU WANT TO FEEL LIKE A BRIDE. The minute you take off your veil, you become a married woman in a white dress.

~ MINIMIZE THE NUMBER OF CHILDREN INCLUDED IN THE WEDDING PARTY.

~ REDEFINE THE WORD "CRISIS." Surprises happen at most weddings, so relax, enjoy, and make the best of things.

~ HIRE A WEDDING COORDINATOR. Planning a wedding is a big job, and if you have the budget or desire to hand the work to a trained professional, by all means, do.

CHAPTER FOUR

The Big Day!

I Do

DRESSING THE HOUSE

At 3:30 in the morning on the day of Kelly's wedding, a clap of thunder rattled my windows and torrents of rain pounded my roof, shattering my sleep. For weeks, we'd been biting our nails as we watched one weather forecast after another calling for rain the day of Kelly's garden wedding. When we were unhappy with the forecast on one TV station or Web site, we flipped to another, hoping for a more favorable prediction.

As one lightning flash after another lit up my room, a jolt of panic shot through me. What were we going to do? Through the months, the wedding guest list had inched its way up. To accommodate the growing crowd, we planned to seat a number of guests in our courtyard, under what we hoped would be a picture-perfect August sky. But if the rain didn't let up, we'd have to squeeze everyone into our home and the event tent set up in our side yard.

Originally, Kelly and I balked at the idea of renting an event tent. I wanted guests to dine and dance under the starry summer night. But when one weatherperson after another predicted stormy skies, we relented and ordered a tent and a dance floor. I'm embarrassed to admit that until then, our "rain plan" consisted of a stand filled with silver-handled umbrellas. Now I was thankful the dry tent stood ready.

As I lay in bed listening to the storm rage, I knew I would not be able to fall back asleep, so I got up and got busy.

A classic procrastinator, I love photo finishes. I have pulled together huge events in a pinch. But I have to admit that decorating my courtyard for the wedding during the pouring rain was stressful even for me. If it hadn't been for my friends, I never would have made it.

The cavalry rode in to save the day as I worked in the wet courtyard, trying not to panic. Cyreesa, my dear friend who manages Nell Hill's, had offered her help in the days leading up to the wedding, but I assured her I had it all under control. A former mother of the bride herself, Cyreesa knew my cool self-assurance would likely melt the morning of the wedding. I'm so thankful she knows me better than I know myself.

In a state of organized chaos, my sister, Judy, decorated; my friend Shirley and her husband, Charlie, built a walkway to get guests across the soupy lawn to the event tent; and others set up tables and pulled together centerpieces.

We cheered when the rain ended just before our guests arrived, and our party could proceed under the stars, just as we had dreamed.

DECKING THE FOYER

When my friend Ann Etienne, a florist from Omaha, Nebraska, arrived early in the morning with a van filled with flowers for the floral arrangements, I had already decorated the banister leading down to the foyer with ropes of gorgeous garlands that Ann made from greens like salal, variegated pit, and seeded eucalyptus. I love to deck our banister with seasonal greens during the holidays, a look Kelly adores, so I knew from experience that fresh garlands are one of the most effective ways to make an ordinary room seem extraordinary. When we decided the ceremony would be held in the foyer, we knew we had to make the stairs stunning. So we asked Ann to make us miles of tangy fresh garlands not only to drape around the banister, but also to hang over our interior doorways, windows, and the front door.

One of my favorites was the still
life we created on the banister
newel post. To give this important spot an air of elegance, I
secured a silver tray to the base
of the banister and then topped
it with an ornate five-armed
silver candelabra. Then Ann
created a floral arrangement
in my friend's antique wedding
compote, and placed it under
the arms of the tall candlestick.
Like a true artist, Ann lets the
container inspire the bouquet.

Festooned with Flowers

Without a doubt, Ann's flower arrangements filled with hot princess roses, stargazer lilies, bells of Ireland, hypericum berries, green hydrangea, buplurum, Kermit mums, and scented geranium leaves stole the show. Since Kelly's goal was for our home to look as if we were hosting a dinner party, we used just a few grand floral arrangements in our foyer and on the dining room table, where the evening's fare would be served.

Since guests would also be gathering in our study and living room, Ann freshened up these rooms with petite bouquets tucked in and among my everyday decor, just as I would if I was hosting a dinner party.

Magical Lighting

One of my favorite tricks when hosting special events is to create magical lighting, both inside and out. And for Kelly's wedding, my home shone as never before. Inside, we filled the house with the most beautiful and ornate candelabras I could find. Then I added votives to nearly every display to give them a twinkling glow.

Outside, we made the yard look like something from a fairy tale by combining a delightful mix of candelabras, chandeliers, and votives. On the posts at the base of the front walkway, we positioned a pair of towering thirteen-armed candelabras, glowing with pillar candles. We clustered groups of votives on each step leading to the front door. Then we suspended wreath chandeliers from the towering shade trees that arch over the front lawn. I love to use wreath chandeliers because they are oh-so-easy to make and they look divine. All you do is lay a standard wreath flat, decorate it with votives, ribbons, and baubles, and then hang it from three thin wires gathered at the top.

Back in our courtyard, we created a backdrop of elegant light by hanging five crystal chandeliers from the canopy of trees that shade the garden. I loved the contrast of the formal lighting hanging against the brick and ivy walls of the garden and how these majestic lights provided soft illumination for the late-night diners.

Next we hung about 150 sparkling votives in a variety of clear glass cups from the branches of the shrubbery that fills the courtyard. I picked several different styles of hanging votive cups, from playful to sophisticated, but used the same creamy white candles to achieve an interesting but harmonious look. To light guests' way from the courtyard to the tent, we lined the path with pillar candles placed in glass hurricanes.

We could not have pulled off this magical lighting without the aid of an army of battery-operated candles. I loved that we could "light" them hours before guests arrived and leave them on long after the event ended without risking a fire. And the fact that they could not be "blown out" by the rain and wind saved the day.

In the side yard, the event tent was luminescent. Sparkling lights glowed just above the netting that created the soft ceiling for this outdoor room. To add to the ambience and provide a bit more light, I hung more wreath chandeliers from the tent's ceiling. These charming wreaths looked so beautiful, no one guessed they were recycled from the holidays, freshened up with summer flowers and greens.

STYLISH CENTERPIECES

Kelly and I decided to dress the dining tables in simple, understated elegance. More than anything, we wanted our guests to enjoy an evening filled with good conversation. So we rented round tables, which would allow guests to easily talk to everyone seated near them, and gold ballroom chairs so we could gather a greater number of guests at each table to make the party merrier.

We covered the tables with a round white undercloth and a cream overlay with satin edging. Then we topped them with a mix of two simple but stylish centerpieces. One treatment featured the

same towering thirteen-armed silver candelabras that welcomed guests as they climbed our front stairway. These ornate fixtures did an amazing job of filling the lofty tent with grandeur. But we knew if we used them on every table, they would overwhelm the space.

So for contrast, we made our second centerpiece treatment smaller and more delicate, but every bit as elegant, by using creamy porcelain two-tiered epergnes. The first time I saw them, I knew these delicate, detailed risers would be ideal as a wedding centerpiece. Each tier of the epergne consisted of four scalloped cups, which we thought made perfect candleholders, so I rested a votive in each one. The top featured a fluted vase, which I filled with sweet bouquets of the same hot pink, lime green, and white flowers used throughout the house.

At the end of the day, when all the tables were dressed and ready, the flower arrangements in place, and the candles lit, I paused for a second to take in the glorious scene. Everything was perfect! With guests due to arrive shortly, it was almost showtime.

SAYING I DO

In the hours before her wedding, Kelly and her bridesmaids were sequestered upstairs in the guest room, away from the chaos that reigned in the house and garden. They sipped champagne and peeked out of the windows at the courtyard, their excitement building as they saw the beautiful scene taking shape below.

In a stroke of genius, Kelly had a makeup artist and hair stylist come to our home to pamper and primp her and her bridesmaids so they would look their best for the celebration. At first, I wasn't sure if having a private salon was worth the investment. But as the pros took charge of the dressing details, Kelly relaxed. I knew then that she had made the right choice.

Downstairs, Britt helped welcome our guests as they arrived. Early in our planning process, Kelly and I decided we wanted guests to be greeted at the door with a warm smile and a glass of bubbly. We chose Prosecco, a sparkling Italian wine that's a high-quality, low-cost alternative to champagne. We set up a table in the center of the foyer and filled it with champagne flutes, lining up the rest of the glasses on the stairway. As soon as the wine was served, we discreetly moved the table to the front patio to make room in the foyer for the ceremony.

As guests milled about the courtyard, enjoying a glass of Prosecco, we treated them to a simple offering of fresh fruit, wedges of aged cheese, and

mixed nuts, all beautifully displayed on silver serving pieces held aloft by iron garden planters. We filled garden urns with ice and stocked them full of wine and bottled water so guests could refresh their drinks.

As the time for the wedding drew near, we ushered our guests to the foyer, which was alive with the delicate music of a classical trio hidden on the second-floor landing. Britt and his groomsmen took their places on the right side of our alcove, next to the Honorable Deanell Tacha, chief justice of the U.S. Court of Appeals for the Tenth Circuit, an old friend of Britt's family who would be performing the ceremony.

We looked up in anticipation as the bridesmaids came down the stairs in turn. As Pachelbel's "Canon in D Major" filled the room, Kelly began her long-anticipated descent to her groom and a sea of well-wishers. The crowd parted as the ladies took their place on the left side of the alcove and turned to face the gentlemen on the other side.

Since the foyer was packed full, we knew it would be hard for everyone to see the ceremony. So after the processional, members of the family stood on the stairs overlooking the bridal party. In order for as many people as possible to get a glimpse of the bride and groom, we hung an ornate mirror on the window frame in the alcove, right behind the wedding party, so all could see their reflection, if not their faces.

During the ceremony, Kelly got misty, so Britt pulled out a handkerchief and tenderly dried her tears. After that, there wasn't a dry eye in the place! That is, until we cheered for joy as the couple kissed for the first time as husband and wife.

The newlyweds exited through our front door, where the photographer waited. And our guests began to file through the dining room, where Cheryl and her assistants had laid out a fabulous feast.

Long before guests arrived, friends helped polish piles of silver trays, cups, and bowls, many of which were family heirlooms, that we would use to serve the hors d'oeuvres and savory dishes. We arranged the serving pieces well ahead of time so they were poised and ready to receive the food, including the three-level, silver cake pedestals that would hold the cupcakes.

Food with a Flourish

Since Kelly's desire was for her wedding to feel like a dinner party, she knew that offering a medley of outstanding dishes was a must. While most brides work hard to select fabulous caterers and sweat over what to include on the menu, for us, this was the easiest part of planning her wedding. We gave full rein to Cheryl, trusting her to pick the perfect selections.

Our only request was to have dishes that could be served at room temperature because there simply wasn't space in my kitchen to heat loads of food or on my dining room table to hold bulky chafing dishes. As we expected, Cheryl worked her culinary magic.

Instead of having a lavish wedding cake, Kelly decided to serve guests cupcakes frosted in white and embellished with the newlyweds' monogram. So as Cheryl contemplated what to serve for the wedding, she took her inspiration from Kelly's cupcakes. She decided to design a feast of petite proportions, presenting a host of foods prepared in individual servings.

THE EVENING'S FARE

Whether she's cooking for guests at her restaurant or for her own family, Cheryl always uses fresh, locally grown, seasonally appropriate foods. And Kelly's late-summer wedding offered her a host of mouthwatering options.

PROSCIUTTO-WRAPPED FILET OF BEEF
Cheryl wrapped individual cuts of steak in thin sheets of prosciutto and then pan-seared them until they were medium rare. She served the entrée with a demiglace and red wine reduction sauce.

SHRIMP AND SCALLOP SHISH KEBABS
After marinating shrimp and scallops in olive oil infused with fresh garlic and herbs, Cheryl combined the seafood with fresh yellow and red pear-shaped tomatoes on a shish kebab skewer. She then lightly grilled the kebabs to give them a light smoky flavor.

Spring green salad in phyllo cups

❧ Cheryl had fun creating these yummy individual salads in crispy phyllo cups. She molded the phyllo pastry into muffin tins and baked them to create the crispy bowls. Then she filled each with a mix of fresh garden greens, blue cheese crumbles, and nuts, all dressed in her signature honey balsamic vinaigrette dressing.

Patty pan squash

❧ These tiny, tasty squash were picked fresh the morning of the wedding and then sautéed in a simple marinade of olive oil, garlic, salt, and pepper.

Green bean bundles

❧ Fresh-picked green beans were first blanched to retain their brilliant green color and crispy texture and then drizzled with a simple vinaigrette dressing with fresh herbs. Then Cheryl bundled small portions of the green beans, tying each with a blanched chive.

Fingerling potatoes with fresh rosemary

❧ Cheryl delicately boiled the freshly harvested potatoes and dressed them in a light sauce of butter, salt, pepper, and fresh rosemary.

Fresh-baked hearty potato bread

❧ Using a family recipe for potato bread as a base, Cheryl added ingredients like caramelized onions, sea salt, and fresh-cracked pepper to make several unique loaves of bread.

The party favors for our guests, little bouquets in silver mint julip cups, were stacked on towering risers throughout the house.

Parting Gifts

After hours of dining, dancing, toasting, and laughing, our guests began to say good-night. As they left our home, we wanted to give them a token of our thanks for joining with us to celebrate Kelly and Britt's union. So we created small party favors we knew they could enjoy in their decorating for years to come. We filled little silver mint julep cups with tiny floral arrangements that mimicked the fabulous flowers that filled the house. And in each bouquet, we tucked in a note of thanks and the newlyweds' at-home information. When the flowers faded, guests could use the cups to hold paper clips, stamps, or other supplies.

Sweet Ending

Building the layers that would hold the cupcakes was a challenge, but we pulled it off. I often have a dramatic display on the large round table that sits between two seating areas in my living room, but this is my favorite one and will always hold sweet memories.

THE DAY ENDS AND MEMORIES TAKE ITS PLACE

The morning after the wedding, when the sun finally broke out after days of rain, we all had to laugh. Despite the monsoon that threatened to capsize our dreams of a garden wedding and the nail-biting scramble to dress our home before guests arrived, Kelly's wedding had been absolutely magical.

While the newlyweds winged their way to a romantic honeymoon in Hawaii, Dan, my sister Judy, and I sat with our feet up at one of the tables under the tent. We were completely exhausted but still glowing from the evening before. The past few months of wedding madness had been wild and creative and full of wonderful moments I'll cherish the rest of my life.

As you begin your journey to "I do," I hope this book helps you savor every moment you spend planning your wedding celebration. My desire is that the tips, techniques, and sage advice I've collected here from the experts will not only reduce your stress as you create the wedding of your dreams, but that they also knit your family closer, as they did mine.

Resources

Most of the accessories featured in this book, unless otherwise noted, are from Mary Carol Garrity's home furnishings stores. For complete information on her stores, visit www.nellhills.com. For additional information on the Mary Carol Home Collection, a complete line of home decor products, contact www.gersoncompany.com for additional information.

NELL HILL'S
501 Commercial Street
Atchison, Kansas 66002
(913) 367-1086
Gifts, accessories, furniture, and tabletop

THE NEW NELL HILL'S
Briarcliff Village
4151 North Mulberry Drive
Kansas City, Missouri 64116
Fabric, bedding, gifts, accessories, furniture, and tabletop

GARRITY'S ENCORE
121 North 5th Street
Atchison, Kansas 66002
(913) 367-1523
Fabric, bedding, gifts, accessories, furniture, and tabletop

This book would not have been possible without the professionals in the field of bridal consultation and event planning (listed on the following page), who contributed many hours and years of experience.

COMPLETE WARDROBE AND EVENT PLANNING

Nolte's Bridal
Proprietor: Michael J. Nolte
- Hawthorne Plaza
  5057 West 119th St.
  Overland Park, Kansas 66209
  (913) 345-1122

- Briarcliff Village
  4149 North Mulberry Drive
  Kansas City, Missouri 64116
  (816) 587-5575
  E-mail: michaeljnolte@aol.com

STATIONERY AND INVITATIONS

RSVP in the Village
Proprietor: Abby Albers
- 3934 West 69th Terrace
  Prairie Village, Kansas 66208
  (913) 432-7787
  E-mail: abby.albers@gmail.com

FOOD AND PASTRIES

- Cakes by Sola
  Proprietor: Rama Sola
  (816) 455-4499
  Page 51

- You Take the Cake
  Proprietor: Kay Benjamin
  (913) 345-2588
  www.takethecakekc.com
  Page 64

- The Vineyards Restaurant
  (Food and Cupcakes)
  Proprietor: Cheryl Hartell
  505 Spring Street
  Weston, Missouri 64098
  816-640-5588

- 3 Women and an Oven
  Proprietors: Jayne Torline, Trish
  Sullivan, and Stacy Webb
  14852 Metcalf Avenue
  Overland Park, Kansas 66223
  Phone: (913) 681-7672
  www.3womendesserts.com
  Pages 62-63, 68, 70

FLORISTS

- Voila!
  Proprietor: Ann Etienne
  4922 Dodge Street
  Omaha, Nebraska 68132
  (402) 991-1970
  www.voilaflowers.com

- The Monarch Flower Company
  Proprietor and Floral Designer:
  Kelly Acock
  By appointment: (913) 636-6961
  www.themonarchflower.com

PHOTOGRAPHY

Bryan E. McCay was the primary book photographer for the Garrity-Bieri wedding. For all other photographs, the pages on which their work appears follows their listings below, and we acknowledge the permission they have granted us to reprint their copyrighted photographs in this book.

- Bryan E. McCay
  (212) 647-1884 or (917) 847-7047
  E-mail: bemcc7@aol.com
  All photography by Bryan E.
  McCay, unless otherwise noted.

- Isaac Alongi Studios
  Proprietor: Isaac Alongi
  2808 West 53rd Street
  Fairway, Kansas 66205-1706
  (913) 236-7304
  ialongi@mac.com
  Pages 30, 31, 34, 35, 36, 37, 51, 56, 57, 72, 73, 74, 83, 84, 86, 87

- Bob Greenspan
  P.O. Box 10413
  Kansas City, Missouri 64171
  (816) 931-2555
  E-mail: bob@bobgreenspan.com
  Front jacket and pages 8, 21 (bottom left), 22, 24-25, 26, 28, 42, 44, 52, 54 (upper left), 58, 62-63, 64, 66, 67, 68, 70, 71, 76, 80, 81, 82, 92, 93

- Mark Hutchinson
  320 Cattleman Trail
  Lawrence, Kansas 66049
  (785) 856-3717
  www.mhutch.com
  E-mail: mhutch01@mac.com
  Pages 44, 97 (lower right), 99, 100

- Bruce L. Snell Photography LLC
  PO Box 4102
  Topeka, Kansas 66604-4102
  (785) 633-7273
  E-mail: bruce@blsphoto.com
  Pages 54 (middle left and bottom left), 55

Acknowledgments

I love working with so many wonderful and creative people who help me make these books possible. I am especially grateful to Jean Lowe, my agent and friend, who worked closely with me to develop the editorial plans for this book. Special thanks to Micki Chestnut, who is able to get all of my thoughts and energy pinned down on paper.

Thank you to the group led by Hugh Andrews and Kirsty Melville at Andrews McMeel Publishing, their staff who did such a beautiful job designing and producing this book: Dorothy O'Brien (editor), Diane Marsh and Julie Barnes (designers), Michelle Daniel, Caty Neis, Julie Roberts, Lesa Reifschneider, Kathy Viele, and Tamara Haus. Thanks to Jennifer Collet, and her marketing team of Kathy Hilliard, Judi Marshall, Rebecca Schuler, and Mackenzie Miller.

I made a new, dear friend when Michael Nolte agreed to offer his expertise, guidance, and name to the book. Michael was kind enough to share his experience on planning and coordinating some of the most beautiful weddings and wardrobes I've seen, including that of Kate Ackerman Jones, and the attire at Amber Krumbholz Schreiber's wedding—both featured in this book.

In addition, I was fortunate to have a great friend in the floral business, Ann Etienne, who went to great lengths to make my home beautiful for Kelly's wedding. Thank you so much! And I'm grateful for my new blooming friendship with florist Kelly Acock, whose work I've admired at the weddings of some close friends. And Cheryl Hartell at The Vineyards in Weston, Missouri, for her incredible friendship and fabulous fare.

Abby Albers at RSVP also helped us out with expert advice on wedding invitations. Kathy Fernholz assisted with photography shoots and sewed some fabulous projects that are featured in these pages. Cynthia and Tom Hoenig graciously opened their home again for our photo shoots. Mary Sullivan, Janet Seeman, and Denise Janes are always there for me; they sure know how to throw a great party! Thanks, too, to Peter and Markie Bieri, not only for the great barbecue celebration, but also for our new son-in-law, Britt.

A special thanks to the brides and their families who brought this book to life by sharing their weddings with us: my dear friends Melanie and David Krumbholz, their daughter Amber and her husband Burt Schreiber, and their darling niece Cassidy Widlowski; for the creative color palettes of Katie Fernholz Pandullo, Kate Ackerman Jones, and Cara Cunningham DeCoursey. And to Kelly's bridal party of John Gravino, Jay Dobbins, Katie McCloskey, and Erica Gregory.

I could not have pulled off the wedding that day without the crises management team of Cyreesa Windsor and Shirley Cline, along with my sister Judy Diebolt, who helped me out in so many ways. I am also grateful to the contributions of stylists Cheryl Owens and Dillon Kinsman and all of the other wonderful, talented employees at Nell Hill's and Garrity's Encore. My dear friends—you know who you are—I am forever grateful.

Finally and fondly, I thank Dan Garrity and Kelly and Britt Bieri for creating wonderful family memories with me.